S0-ARC-376

XXX HOLY~
JOURNEYS
INTO THE
SPIRITUAL
HEART OF
INDIA

XXX HOLY~ JOURNEYS INTO THE SPIRITUAL HEART OF INDIA

PHOTOGRAPHS BY
PETER BIALOBRZESKI
WITH ESSAYS BY
FLORIAN HANIG
AND MICK BROWN

»When I saw this image on my contact sheet, I knew there is something to explore. The result of this investigation is this book.«

GÖTTERGEWIMMEL

von Florian Hanig

Gott ist nicht tot in Indien. Im Taxi vom Flughafen in die Stadt
thront er auf dem Armaturenbrett, ein kleiner Plastik-Krishna,
bunte Glühbirnen flackern hinter seinem Kopf, im Aschenbecher
zu seinen Füßen glühen Sandelholzstäbchen. Die Rauchschlieren
vermischen sich mit der schweren heißen Luft, die durch die Wagen-
fenster weht. Am Abend tanzt er über die Bühne, umringt von Frauen
mit aufgerissenen, kohleumrandeten Augen und langen Fingern, als
Elefantengott, mit Blumengirlanden umhängt wie eine hawaiische
Schönheit. Er ist unter den Ersten, die im Morgennebel auf den
Tempeltreppen im Ganges stehen und das Wasser in beiden Händen
der Sonne entgegenstrecken, es über Kopf und Körper perlen lassen.
Er wacht über die Kinder, die kleine Papierboote mit Kerzen und
Wünschen beladen in den Fluß setzen. Und wenn die hageren Kühe
in den engen Gassen von Benares ihren Kot aus ihrem Hintern
bröckeln lassen, stört auch das niemanden; es ist „holy shit".

Gott ist überall in Indien. Auf den Lastwagen steht in großen
bunten Lettern „God is great, please honk, Tata, Tata", in den
Straßen verstecken sich kleine Schreine, deren Steinfiguren von so
vielen Fingern berührt, von so vielen Hoffnungen blankgescheuert
wurden, dass nur noch runde Knubbelmännchen geblieben sind.

Das Göttliche durchdringt alle Orte und alle Geschehen, und
dieser Spiritualität kann sich kein Reisender in Indien entziehen –
besonders wenn er aus einem Land kommt, in dem Religion am
Rand der Gesellschaft stattfindet, wo Gott in einem Gotteshaus sitzt
und nur sonn- und feiertags als spiritueller Dienstleister besucht
wird, von einer immer kleiner werdenden Gruppe.

Diese Spiritualität ist Teil der Bilder auf den folgenden Seiten. Wir
spüren sie, auch wenn wir den Glauben nicht verstehen, wenn die
Sanskrit-Lehren für uns nur eine Ansammlung von Zungenbrechern
bleiben, der Hindu-Pantheon sich als Gewirr aus Vielärmlern und
Rüsselschwenkern darstellt, uns die Religion manchmal als Freak-
show erschreckt: mit Sadhus, die jahrelang auf einem Bein stehen,
und Gurus, die Askese aus ihrem Rolls Royce predigen.

Der erste Priester, den ich in Indien traf, wollte mir Haschisch
verkaufen. Er war ein kleiner, schwitzender Mann mit zwei roten
Kreidestrichen auf seiner Stirn und einem Lächeln ohne Schneide-
zähne. Nachdem wir weder eine „special puja" bezahlen wollten
noch eine Tour durch den Tempel (sein Englisch war miserabel), zog
er einen kleinen Beutel mit braunen Krümeln aus seinem „dhoti"
und strahlte. Ein Priester als Dealer! Ich fand das unmöglich, meine

indischen Verwandten zuckten mit den Schultern. Es gibt keine streng geführten Konfessionen in Indien, keine Glaubenskongregationen und keine Exkommunikation. Jeder kann sich Guru (Lehrer) nennen oder Swami (Heiliger), er muß nur genug andere finden, die ihm folgen. Jahre später sah ich, wie Priester in einem Tempel in Saundatti junge Mädchen der Göttin Yellamma weihten. Bezahlt wurden sie von Zuhältern, denn die Weihe machte die Mädchen zu Tempelhuren. Das war die erste Erfahrung: Es gibt keine Kirche im Hinduismus.

Die zweite war: Es gibt keinen Hinduismus. Es gibt Zigtausende. Meine Schwiegermutter betet Tara an, eine weibliche Inkarnation des Buddha, meine Frau hat den Elefantengott Ganesh und den Hirtenjungen Krishna auf unser Fensterbrett gestellt. Mein Schwiegervater kennt zwar die Epen so gut wie kein anderer in der Familie und befolgt die Rituale, doch er glaubt nur an eine abstrakte göttliche Macht, nicht an einzelne Götter. Trotzdem sind sie alle Hindus. Und unser Fahrer in Bangalore verwandelt den Suzuki der Schwiegereltern in einen Tempel zu Ehren Shivas, mit Girlanden um den Spiegel und Aschepunkten auf Lenkrad und Zündschloß (ein Schutz, auf den er vertraut, im Gegensatz zum Sicherheitsgurt, den er nicht anrührt).

330 Millionen Götter soll es in Indien geben, also beinahe so viele, wie es Einwohner in Europa gibt. Statistisch gesehen kommt ein Gott auf je drei Einwohner (zieht man die Christen, Muslime, Parsen und Sikhs ab, deren paar Götter zahlenmäßig nicht ins Gewicht fallen, dann teilen sich sogar je zwei Hindus einen Gott!). Die spirituelle Versorgung ist also weitaus besser als die medizinische (ein Arzt versorgt 2 500 Menschen) und die schulische (knapp zwei Drittel aller Frauen können nicht lesen!).

Einige der Götter sind Megastars, stehen in jedem zweiten oder dritten Tempel, Shiva zum Beispiel, der Zerstörer und Erneuerer, Vishnu, der Bewahrer, oder Lakshmi, die Göttin des Wohlstands. Akademiker haben ein Faible für Ganesh, den Elefantengott, der sich einen seiner Stoßzähne abbrach, um die großen Epen aufzuschreiben, und viele Frauen himmeln Krishna an, den Verführer Zehntausender Hirtenmädchen und romantischen Flötenspieler. Daneben gibt es lokale Größen wie die zornige Kali, die überall in Kalkutta den Menschen ihre blutrote Zunge rausstreckt und im Vergleich zu deren Fratze alles Elend dieser Metropole erträglich wird. Einige Dorfgötter genießen nur über ein paar Weilern die Lufthoheit.

Sowenig es allgemeingültige Götter gibt, sowenig gibt es allgemein verbindliche Gebote. Die Jains, Mitglieder einer hinduistischen Sekte, nehmen das Gebot „Du sollst nicht töten" so ernst, daß sie sich Tücher vor den Mund binden, um keine Mücken einzuatmen. Ihre Priester gehen nackt, um keine Wesen in ihren Kleidern zu zerdrücken. Und etwa die Hälfte aller Hindus sind strikte Vegetarier. Die andere Hälfte findet Tandoori-Hühnchen klasse.

Die Epen, die Mahabharata und die Ramayana, enthalten keine Handlungsvorschriften, sondern sind eine Sammlung von Geschichten, die sich vielfältig widersprechen, einmal Shiva zum höchsten Gott erheben, ein anderes Mal den abstrakten Brahma, dann wieder Vishnu. Es sind Geschichten, die vor zwei- bis dreitausend Jahren geschrieben wurden und die heute noch lebendig sind. Vor ein paar Jahren strahlte das staatliche Fernsehen die Ramayana als 140folgige Serie aus; zur Sendezeit konnte man damals in Bombay oder Delhi kein Taxi bekommen, sammelten sich in den Bazaren Trauben vor den Fernsehern. Gefilmt wurden die Streifen in Bollywood, wie die Filmstudios in Bombay verballhornt werden. Die Götter trugen Kunstpelzwamse und warfen – selbst auf dem ältesten Schwarzweiß-fernseher noch deutlich zu sehen – Felsbrocken aus Pappmaché. Doch der Glaube war stärker als die Raffinesse der Trickfilmtechnik. Die Großmutter einer Freundin, die in ihren letzten Lebensjahren alle Folgen der Ramayana auf Video im Zimmer gehortet hatte, betete vor dem Fernseher.

Ohne diesen festen Glauben, glaube ich, ist Indien nicht zu ertragen. Vor dem Taj Mahal habe ich mich einmal mit einem Rikschafahrer gestritten, der nicht von meiner Seite wich und darauf bestand, morgen zu meinem Hotel zu kommen. „Maybe tomorrow, Sahib", wiederholte er in einem fort. „Maybe next trip." „Maybe next life", antwortete ich genervt. Er spuckte aus und sagte: „Next life, you will be rikshaw driver. And I will be tourist."

Der Glaube erklärt auch, weshalb fast eine halbe Milliarde Menschen sich in unwürdigster Armut abrackern und den paar Millionen unter ihnen, die in verschwenderischem Luxus leben, nicht den Hals umdrehen. Das Schicksal jedes einzelnen sehen Hindus als Akkumulation guter oder schlechter Taten in den vorherigen Leben. Jede Profession und jede dazugehörige Kaste trägt ihre eigenen Verhaltensnormen mit sich: nicht nur, was gute und schlechte Taten sind, sondern auch, wie man zu beten hat, welches Essen erlaubt ist, wer wen heiraten darf, die Farbe der Kleidung, das Verhalten der Eltern gegenüber ihren Kindern usw. Die Brahmanen, Mitglieder der hohen Priesterkaste, sollen zum Beispiel nicht scharf essen, um die Begierden zu zügeln, und Kleidung tragen, die möglichst nicht genäht ist, die niedrigstehenden Sudras kein Essen für Brahmanen kochen. Rollenwechsel sind nicht vorgesehen: In der Bhagavadgita sagt Vishnu, daß jeder Mensch seine Standespflicht erfüllen müsse. Selbst wenn ein Bauer als Feldherr einen Sieg erringt, ist dies so kein gottgefälliges Verhalten, weil er sich gegen die kosmische Ordnung gesetzt hat. Wer dagegen als Latrinenreiniger seinen Job ohne Murren erfüllt, der sammelt Karma-Punkte auf dem Schicksalskonto und kann mit einer Wiedergeburt in einer höheren Kaste rechnen. Natürlich ist das eine sehr, sehr grobe Verkürzung des Kastensystems und der Inkarnationslehre, und die Wirklichkeit ist vielschichtiger: Ein Unberührbarer ist heute Präsident in Delhi, und Diskriminierung aufgrund der Kastenherkunft ist strafbar. In den Werbeagenturen und Computerfirmen in Bombay, Madras oder Kalkutta fragt heute niemand mehr nach der Kaste des einzelnen, ist die Heirat über Kastengrenzen hinweg kein Thema mehr. Doch in den kleinen Städten und den Dörfern Indiens, von denen es eine Million gibt, unterdrückt das Kastenwesen die Ambitionen der Armen und verschafft den Wohlhabenden ein reines Gewissen. Oder, wie mir ein Freund aus Dehli gesagt hat: „Inder bist du erst, wenn du über hundert Bettler hinwegsteigen kannst, ohne mit der Wimper zu zucken."

Und noch auf eine andere Weise hilft der Glaube, das Elend auszublenden: die einbeinigen Bettler, die Mädchen mit den großen Kulleraugen, die vor dem Autofenster mit der Hand zum Mund fahren, die Wellblechhütten entlang der Runways der Flughäfen – alles Täuschung, „maya", Illusion. Wie du, lieber Leser. Wie dieses Buch. Der Mensch ist für Hindus Teil des göttlichen Einen, des Brahman, und seine Existenz nur eine Täuschung, die er überwinden muß. „Moksha", die Erlösung, ist erst nach unzähligen Wiedergeburten zu erreichen, durch eine endgültige Erkenntnis, die die Illusion der Welt durchschaut. (Auch das ist natürlich nur eine grobe Verkürzung.)

Die Weltabgewandtheit des Hinduismus kann ungemein frustrieren: Verabredungen, Fahrpläne, alles wird, wenn nicht als „maya" gesehen, so doch zumindest so behandelt. Niemand repariert die Telefonleitungen, füllt die Löcher in den Straßen, wozu auch. Das Heil liegt nicht im Irdischen. Diese Weltabgewandtheit erhebt dieses Land aber auch über alle anderen: Eine Frau im grünen Sari, die in ihrer Hütte auf der Müllkippe Kalkuttas sitzt, aufrecht, das Haar zum Knoten gedreht und mit einem Gesicht wie eine Madonna von Riemenschneider, ein kleiner Junge, der mit sechs Gläsern dampfenden Tees im Drahtgestell durch die Markthallen Bombays läuft, Schafhirten, die sich aus dem Staub der Wüste lösen, die Männer mit leuchtenden Turbanen, die Frauen in Saris voll funkelnder Spiegel – es gibt diese Momente in Indien, da glaubt man, von göttlichen Wesen umgeben zu sein, die hier ein paar absurde Rollen spielen, ohne richtig bei der Sache zu sein, denn sie haben ihren Blick schon längst auf etwas gerichtet, das so wunderschön ist, daß wir es nur an ihrem Lächeln erahnen können.

Florian Hanig hat vier Jahre lang bei „MERIAN" als Redakteur die Asienhefte betreut. Heute arbeitet er für „GEO Special".

PROFUSION OF GODS

by Florian Hanig

God is not dead in India. He sits regally on the dashboard of the taxi going from the airport to the city centre. Fairy lights flicker behind the head of this little plastic Krishna. Sandalwood joss sticks glow in the ashtray at his feet. The ribbons of smoke issuing from them curl into the hot, heavy air wafting in from the window. At night he dances on stage. Women with long fingers and large, kohl-rimmed eyes circle around him. He is an elephant god hung with garlands of flowers like a Hawaiian beauty. He is one of the first to be found standing in the morning mist on the temple stairs in the Ganges. One of the first to lift water in cupped hands towards the sun and let it trickle down onto his head and body. He watches over children setting little paper boats adrift into the river laden with candles and wishes. And nobody seems to mind emaciated cows dropping their dung in the narrow alleys of Benares: their shit is holy.

God is everywhere in India. Huge, colourful letters emblazoned across the lorries announce "God is great, please honk, tata tata". Tiny shrines are hidden in the streets. Their statues have been stroked by so many fingers, have been sanded smooth by so many hopes, that nothing is left of them but stumpy, round, Michelin-man like figurines.

The divine saturates everything and anything that goes on. No traveller to India can remain oblivious to this spirituality – particularly if he or she comes from a country where religion has been relegated to the periphery of society. Countries where God sits in his appointed house and only receives custom on Sundays and holidays from a group of people that is continually shrinking in numbers.

This spirituality is an element of the photographs on the ensuing pages. We can sense it even if we do not understand their faith. We can feel it even if Sanskrit dogma remains a litany of tongue-twisters for us, and the Hindu pantheon presents itself as a confusion of many-armed creatures, some depicted with elephant-like trunks frozen in motion. Even if the religion puts us off because it looks a bit like a freak show: the Sadhus that stand on one leg for years, the gurus that preach poverty from inside their Rolls Royces.

The first priest I met in India wanted to sell me some hash. He was a small, sweaty man with two red chalk circles on his forehead and a grin that showed the gaps where his eye teeth used to be. When we declined to pay for a special puja and to take a tour of the temple (his English was appalling), he pulled a small pouch filled with brown nuggets out of his dhoti and beamed. A priest doubling as a dealer! I was shocked, but my Indian relative just shrugged his shoulders. No denominations are strictly adhered to in India. There are no congregations of believers and no such thing as excommunication. Anyone can call himself a guru (teacher) or a swami (saint) – he just has to find enough disciples. Years later I witnessed a priest initiating young girls into the service of the goddess Yellamma in a temple in Saundatti. This was paid for by their pimps. Their initiation elevated the girls to the whores of the temple. This was the initial experience: there is no church in Hinduism.

The second one was this: there is no Hinduism as such. There are thousands of Hinduisms. My mother-in-law prays to Tara, a female incarnation of the Buddha. My wife places the elephant god Ganesh and the shepherd boy Krishna on our windowsill. My father-in-law knows the epic poems better than anyone else in the family and observes their rituals, but he still believes only in an abstract, divine power, not in individual gods. Despite this they are all Hindus. And our driver in Bangalore transformed my in-laws' Suzuki into a temple in honour of Shiva. He draped garlands around the rear-view mirror and dotted ashes on the handlebars and the ignition (the only safety precaution he trusts – he never touches the safety belt).

Apparently there are 330 million gods in India – almost as many as people who live in Europe. This works out to a god for every three people in India. And, if you take away the Christians, Parsees and Sikhs, whose few gods hardly make a difference in the calculation, then there is a god for every two Hindus! Spiritual guidance is therefore a great deal more widespread than either medical (there is only one doctor for every 2,500 people) or educational (nearly two thirds of all the women are illiterate).

Some of the gods are true megastars and can be found in every second or third temple. Shiva, for example, the great destroyer and giver of new life. Vishnu, the guardian. Lakshmi, the goddess of wealth. Academicians have a weak spot for Ganesh, the elephant god who broke off one of his tusks to write the great epic poems. And lots of women adore Krishna, the romantic piper and seducer of tens of thousands of shepherdesses. Then there are the big local gods like the enraged Kali who sticks his blood-red tongue out at people everywhere in Calcutta. After seeing his hideous face, all the rest of the hardship in this metropolis seems bearable by comparison. And some village gods only enjoy sovereignty over a few hamlets.

Just as there are very few universally worshipped gods, there are also very few universally accepted commandments. The Jains, members of a Hindu sect, take the commandment "Thou shalt not kill" so seriously that they bind a cloth in front of their mouths so as not to inhale any flies by mistake. Their priests go naked so that they do not crush any small creatures in their clothing. And about one third of all Hindus are strict vegetarians. The rest think tandoori chicken is fantastic.

The epic poems, the Mahabharata and the Ramayana, are not receptacles of rules of behaviour but collections of stories that frequently contradict themselves. One exalts Shiva as the most important god. Another gives this honour to Brahma, and yet another to Vishnu. They are stories that were written two to three thousand years ago, but they are still very much alive today. A few years ago the state television station broadcast the Ramayana as a 140-episode series. While it was shown you could not get a taxi in Bombay or New Delhi, and clusters of people collected in front of the televisions in the bazaars. It was filmed in Bollywood – the Indian slang term for the film studios in Bombay. The gods wore faux fur waistcoats and tossed about fake stones made of papier maché – undeniably obvious even on the most ancient of black-and-white televisions. But belief proved stronger than the flawed finesse of film technique. The grandmother of a friend of mine, who hoarded the videos of all of the episodes of the Ramayana in her room, prayed in front of the television.

I am convinced that, in the lack of this unshakeable belief, India would be impossible to come to grips with. I once had a row with a rickshaw driver in front of the Taj Mahal. He was glued to my side and insisted upon coming to my hotel the next day. "Maybe tomorrow, Sahib", he kept saying. "Maybe next trip." "Maybe next life", I said in annoyance. He spat and said, "Next life you will be rickshaw driver. And I will be tourist."

This belief also explains why almost half a billion human beings toil away in abject poverty and do not wring the necks of the few million who live in lavish luxury. Hindus regard the fate of every individual as the accumulated result of good or bad deeds in their past lives. Each profession and accompanying caste adheres to its own norms of behaviour that dictate not only what is good and bad but also how its members are to pray, what foods are allowed, whom one may marry, the colour of their clothes, the parents' attitude toward their children, etc. The Brahmans, members of the highest class of priests, may not eat spicy food so that they can keep their desires in check, and must try not to wear clothes that have been sewn. The Sudras, who are lower in standing, may not cook for Brahmans. An exchange of roles is not permissible. In the Bhagavadgita Vishnu says that every human being has to fulfil the responsibilities dictated to him by his social standing. Even if a peasant achieves a victory as a commander on the battlefield, this is not behaviour the gods would smile upon: he has defied the cosmic order of the universe. But someone who does his duty as a cleaner of toilets without complaining collects karma points in the cosmic account of his fate and can expect to be reborn in a higher caste.

This is of course a very simplified view of the caste system and teaching of reincarnation – the reality is much more complex. An Untouchable is currently the President in Delhi, and discrimination by caste is illegal. Nobody in the advertising agencies and computer companies in Bombay, Madras or Calcutta would ever ask about an individual's caste these days, and marriage between different castes is no longer an issue. But still, in the millions of India's small towns and villages, the caste system continues to suppress the ambitions of the poor and gives the wealthy a clear conscience. Or, as a friend in Delhi said to me: "You'll only truly be an Indian when you can step over a hundred beggars without batting an eyelash."

Belief also helps to blind people to poverty in another way. The one-legged beggars, the little girls with their big eyes who put their hands to their mouths in front of your car windows, the corrugated iron huts flanking the runways at the airport – this is all a deception, maya, an illusion. Just like you are, dear reader. Just like this book. For Hindus, human beings are only a small part of the divine One. The Brahman and his existence are only an illusion that he must get beyond. Moksha – salvation – can only be reached after countless reincarnations, through the final realisation that exposes the illusion that is our world. (This of course is also a gross simplification.)

This Hindu withdrawal from the material world can frustrate you terribly. Appointments, public transport schedules – even if they are not regarded as maya they are still treated as if they were. Nobody repairs telephone lines, fills in potholes in the streets – why should they? There is no real good in earthly things. But it is also this withdrawal from the material that exalts this country above all others. A woman in a green sari sits in front of her hut on the rubbish tip in Calcutta – she sits tall, her hair twisted into a bun, with a face like a Riemenschneider madonna. A small boy runs through the market halls of Bombay carrying six glasses of steaming tea in a wire frame. Shepherds materialise as the desert dust settles: men wearing bright turbans, women in saris glittering with mirrors… There are these moments in India in which you feel surrounded by divine spirits playing absurd roles without taking much notice of what they are doing. They have long since directed their gaze toward something else that is so indescribably beautiful that we can only begin to imagine it by observing their quiet smiles.

Florian Hanig worked for "MERIAN" for 4 years as the editor of the Asia editions. He is currently working for "GEO Special".

SPIRITUAL TOURISTS

by Mick Brown

In 1932 the English writer and seeker Paul Brunton undertook his first visit to India in search of the key to its sacred wisdom. Pausing in Benares, Brunton was struck by a moment of intense revelation. "So this", he wrote, "is India's holiest city! Well, it possesses a most unholy smell! Is it not better to be an errant infidel and breathe clean air than acquire piety at such a monstrous price? Benares! You may be the hub of Hindu culture, yet please learn something from the infidel whites and temper your holiness with hygiene!"

Manfully holding his nose, Brunton persevered. His travels through India eventually led him to the ashram of the great Tamil saint, Ramana Maharishi, to whom Brunton remained a devotee for the rest of his life. The paradoxes of India – the heat, the physical discomforts, the beauty, the chaos (not to mention the sanitation) which can make it maddening, magical, exhilerating and exhausting by turns, have proved no deterrent to infidel whites, like Brunton, in search of enlightenment.

The early part of the twentieth century saw a procession of like-minded spiritual tourists heading east. There was the Russian painter Nicholas Roerich; the French Tibetologist Alexandra Graham-Neel, and the Russian occultist, Madame Helena Blavatsky, who founded the Theosophical Society, with the specific intention of unifying Eastern and Western philosophy into a religion for the new age. There was W. Evans-Wentz, an American, who was responsible for the first Western translation of Tibetan Buddhist funerary rites, popularised as "The Tibetan Book of the Dead"; and Sir Edwin Arnold, a British colonial educationalist whose years spent running colleges in India stimulated an interest in orientalism which result-ed in him writing his epic poem about the Buddha, "The Light of Asia", which was a bestseller in Britain and America.

The drug-culture of the Sixties precipitated a massive migration to the East of young people disaffected with the values of their own culture, and hoping to find some antidote to Western materialism in the Eastern spiritual traditions – a migration which continues unabated today.

One may see these spiritual tourists travelling everywhere in India, thronging railway platforms and bus stations, clutching copies of the Lonely Planet; lingering at the ghats of Varanasi or Haridwar; queuing for darshan in the Puttaparthi ashram of the venerated guru Sai Baba, or in Dharamsala for a public audience with the Dalai Lama.

India's religious tradition is vast and complex, and, at first glance, dauntingly impenetrable. The Hindu pantheon contains one creator but thousands of subsidiary deities – four-armed gods, voluptuous goddesses, elephant and monkey gods – their names often changing from region to region, each with their own story. Embroidered together they create a dazzling mythology of creation, birth, life and death and every facet of mankind's aspirations, failings and triumphs. To step into this mythology is to immerse oneself in the river of life.

At its essence is an abiding sense of the holiness of all things. Here, spirituality is not separate from man, something to be observed in empty ritual at specific times in specific places; it is at the core of every activity and every moment. It is the pilgrims painstakingly circumambulating Mount Arunchala, the heart chakra of the body of India; it is the woman on the banks of the Ganges at Rishikesh, carefully shaping a small boat of palm leaves and flowers, with a stick of incense as a mast, and launching it into the river, a vessel for her prayers; it is the ornate religious symbol sketched in coloured chalk on a pavement in Pondicherry; the "om" signs and swastikas which decorate every Tata truck, hauling their loads down the Punjab roads.

To the spiritual tourist, this unending religious pageant can be as baffling as it is magical, and yet simply to bear witness to it is to be offered a glimpse of a connection between man and spirit which has been largely lost in the West. The very act of travelling through India can, in itself, seem like a test of the spirit; the constant demands on one's time, attention and charity, the mixture of kindness and indifference; one quickly learns to shed one's western skin and the attitudes that come with it, or go mad. For better or worse, India changes people.

For most Westerners, engagement with the spiritual traditions of India comes in the person of a particular guru or teacher. The ashrams of Rishikesh are filled with Western students, tranced out in meditation or bent double in their attempts to master yoga. In Bombay, students queue for an audience with Ramesh, a former bank manager who is now recognised as the great master of advaita teachings.

At Sai Baba's ashram in Puttaparthi, organised parties arrive from every corner of the world, many of them uniformly dressed in white, with neckerchiefs denoting their country of origin, to sit for hours in the dust outside the mandir, awaiting darshan with Baba. So numerous are the crowds of pilgrims that flock to Puttaparthi that the ashram has been obliged to build its own airstrip; so copious the flow of donations that Baba has established schools, built the most sophisticated hospital in India and still had enough left to lay water supplies to the villages throughout the state.

Mingling with the crowds at Puttaparthi one is aware that here is to be found every facet of humanity; the faithful, the pious, the desperate, the hopeful, the greedy, the healthy and the afflicted – all human life drawn to the promise of deliverance or gain.

Encountering Sai Baba requires an enormous leap of faith, if one is to believe the claims of his devotees, and Baba himself, that he is an avatar, a living incarnation of the divine. There is no institutionalised hierarchy to arbitrate in such matters: a guru's divinity is measured by his teachings and his actions and the faith of his devotees. Nor, of course, are there any guarantees. The history of the West's engagement with Indian spirituality is littered with the stories of the broken promises of messiahs and the shattered expectations of devotees. Discernment is the spiritual tourist's most indispensable tool. On his travels in India in the 1930s, Paul Brunton encountered Meher Baba, a guru who would later attract a large following in the West, and who had no hesitation in claiming that he was "the avatar of the age". Brunton concluded that Meher Baba was certainly deluded and possibly mad.

But perhaps the most salutory, and poignant, example of this curious relationship between East and West is the story of Krishnamurti. Walking on the beach at Adyar, near Madras, one day in 1909, the English Theosophist Charles Leadbeater caught sight of a 12-year-old boy whose aura, Leadbeater divined, was "devoid of any particle of selfishness". Leadbeater and his fellow Theosophist Annie Besant spent the next 20 years grooming Krishnamurti as the new "World Teacher" – only for Krishnamurti to turn on them and reject the role.

It is an evocative experience to walk on that same beach at Adyar where Leadbeater discovered his young protégé and to reflect on the perennial Western belief that spiritual deliverance is to be found in the East, and the disappointments that may result. The pure white sand runs down to a sparkling turquoise sea, the sunlight playing on the surface. A group of young boys make their way along the water's edge and, spying a foreigner, change tack and trudge across the sand to engage in conversation. What is your name?, they want to know. Where have you come from? What are you doing here? The mention of the name Krishnamurti means nothing to them. The idea that anyone should travel from the West to this place in search of enlightenment strikes them as implausible, absurd. For them, the West is the promised land – a place of motor-cycles and pop music, of jobs where they will earn good money. "It is where I dream of going", says one.

Krishnamurti, too, went West. Rejecting his annointed role as the World Teacher with the famous words that "truth is a pathless land", and that each man must find his own deliverance, he moved to California. The air, he said, was cleaner there.

Mick Brown is the author of the bestselling book "The Spiritual Tourist" and writes regulary for the London based "Telegraph Magazine".

Spirituelle Touristen

von Mick Brown

1932 unternahm der englische Schriftsteller und Suchende Paul Brunton seine erste Reise nach Indien, auf der Suche nach dem Schlüssel zur heiligen Weisheit des Landes. Bei einem Aufenthalt in Benares überkam es Brunton wie eine Offenbarung. „Dies also ist Indiens heiligste Stadt", schrieb er. „Sie stinkt zum Himmel! Ist es nicht besser, ein fehlgeleiteter Ungläubiger zu sein und saubere Luft zu atmen, als für den Erwerb von Frömmigkeit einen derart horrenden Preis zahlen zu müssen? Benares! Du bist vielleicht der Mittelpunkt der indischen Kultur, aber bitte lerne etwas von den weißen Ungläubigen und mäßige deine Heiligkeit durch Hygiene!"

Brunton hielt sich tapfer die Nase zu und ließ sich nicht beirren. Seine Reisen durch Indien führten ihn schließlich zum Ashram des großen tamilischen Heiligen Ramana Maharishi, dessen Anhänger er bis zum Ende seines Lebens bleiben sollte. Die Widersprüche Indiens – die Hitze, die Unbequemlichkeiten, die Schönheit, das Chaos (ganz zu schweigen von der Hygiene), die abwechselnd unerträglich, berauschend, verzaubernd und anstrengend sein können – konnten ungläubige Weiße, die, wie Brunton, auf der Suche nach Erleuchtung waren, nicht abschrecken.

Der Beginn des zwanzigsten Jahrhunderts erlebte eine Prozession gleichgesinnter spiritueller Touristen, die es gen Osten zog. So den russischen Maler Nicholas Roerich, die französische Tibetologin Alexandra Graham-Neel und die russische Okkultistin Madame Helena Blavatsky, die die Theosophische Gesellschaft mit dem ausdrücklichen Ziel gegründet hatte, östliche und westliche Philosophien zur Religion eines neuen Zeitalters zu vereinen. Zu nennen wäre auch der Amerikaner W. Evans-Wentz, dem die erste Übersetzung tibetisch-buddhistischer Bestattungsriten zu verdanken ist, die als „Tibetanisches Totenbuch" weite Verbreitung gefunden hat. Schließlich ist der Kolonialbeamte Sir Edwin Arnold zu erwähnen, jener britische Pädagoge, dessen Jahre als Schulleiter in Indien in ihm das Interesse für den Orientalismus weckten, das ihn schließlich zu seinem Epos über Buddha inspirierte. Unter dem Titel „The Light of Asia" wurde das Buch in Großbritannien und Amerika zum Bestseller.

Die Drogenkultur der sechziger Jahre löste eine regelrechte Völkerwanderung nach Osten aus. Junge Leute, die mit den Wertvorstellungen der eigenen Gesellschaft unzufrieden waren, hofften, in den spirituellen Traditionen des Ostens ein Gegenmittel zum westlichen Materialismus zu finden. Dieser Zustrom hält bis heute unvermindert an.

Solche spirituellen Touristen, den alternativen Reiseführer „Lonely Planet" in der Hand, findet man in Indien überall, auf Bahnsteigen und in Busbahnhöfen, an den Ufertreppen in Varanasi oder Haridwar. Sie stehen Schlange vor dem Ashram in Puttaparthi für ein Darshan des verehrten Grurus Sai Baba oder in Dharamsala für eine öffentliche Audienz beim Dalai Lama.

Indiens religiöse Tradition ist so groß und komplex, daß sie auf den ersten Blick beängstigend unzugänglich wirkt. Im Pantheon der Hindus gibt es einen Schöpfer, aber Tausende untergeordneter Gottheiten – vierarmige Götter, üppige Göttinnen, Elefanten- und Affengötter, deren Namen sich oft von Region zu Region unterscheiden und von denen jeder seine eigene Geschichte hat. Miteinander verwoben, bilden sie eine verwirrende Mythologie der Schöpfung, von Geburt, Leben und Tod, die jede Facette menschlicher Ziele, menschlicher Niederlagen und Triumphe abdeckt. In diese Mythologie einzutauchen gleicht einem Bad im Fluß des Lebens.

Im Zentrum steht der unvergängliche Glaube daran, daß alle Dinge heilig sind, denn hier ist die Spiritualität nicht vom Menschen losgelöst, sie ist nicht nur ein leeres Ritual, das man zu ganz bestimmten Zeiten an ganz bestimmten Orten begeht, sie liegt im Kern jeder Handlung und jeder Bewegung. Sie ist in den Pilgern, die gewissenhaft den Mount Arunchala umrunden, das Herz-Chakra Indiens; sie ist in den Frauen, die am Ufer des Ganges in Rishikesh aus Palmenblättern und Blumen ein kleines Boot bauen, mit einem Räucherstäbchen als Mast, das sie, angefüllt mit ihren Gebeten, auf den Fluß aussetzen; sie ist in dem kunstvollen religiösen Symbol, das in Pondicherry mit Kreide auf den Bürgersteig gemalt ist, in den Om-Zeichen und Hakenkreuzen, die im Punjab jeden schwerbeladenen Tata-Truck schmücken.

Auf den spirituellen Touristen kann diese nicht enden wollende religiöse Fülle ebenso verwirrend wie magisch wirken, und doch empfindet er es wie ein Geschenk, sie miterleben zu dürfen, wie einen Blick auf die Verbindung zwischen Mensch und Geist, die im Westen längst verlorengegangen ist. Eine Reise durch Indien kann einer Prüfung für den Geist gleichen, so groß ist der Anspruch an Zeit, Aufmerksamkeit und Wohltätigkeit, so stark der Eindruck, den die Mischung aus Freundlichkeit und Gleichgültigkeit hinterläßt; man lernt schnell, seine westliche Haut und die dazugehörigen Einstellungen abzustreifen, oder man wird verrückt. Indien verändert den Menschen, zum Guten oder zum Schlechten.

Für die meisten Menschen aus dem Westen ist das Interesse an den spirituellen Traditionen Indiens mit der Person eines bestimmten Gurus oder Lehrers verbunden. Die Ashrams in Rishikesh sind voll von westlichen Studenten, die in meditativer Trance verharren oder sich bei einer Joga-Übung verrenken. In Bombay stehen die Studenten Schlange für einen Audienz bei Ramesh, einem früheren Bankmanager, der heute als der große Meister der Advaita-Lehre anerkannt ist.

Sai Babas Ashram in Puttaparthi ist das Ziel organisierter Reisegruppen aus der ganzen Welt, viele von ihnen einheitlich in Weiß gekleidet, mit unterschiedlichen Halstüchern, je nach Herkunftsland, die stundenlang vor dem Mandir im Staub sitzen und auf ein Darshan bei Baba warten. So zahlreich sind die Pilger, die nach Puttaparthi strömen, daß der Ashram eine eigene Landebahn anlegen mußte; so großzügig sind die Spenden, daß Baba Schulen gründen und das modernste Krankenhaus in Indien bauen lassen konnte. Danach war immer noch genug Geld übrig, um die Dörfer des Bundesstaates an die Wasserversorgung anzuschließen.

Wenn man sich in Puttaparthi unter die Pilger mischt, wird man sich bewußt, daß hier der Mensch in seiner ganzen Vielfalt versammelt ist: Treue und Fromme, Verzweifelte und Hoffnungsvolle, Habgierige, Gesunde und Kranke. Das gesamte Spektrum des menschlichen Lebens, angezogen von der verheißenden Erlösung oder vom erhofften Profit.

Ob man Sai Baba und seinen Anhängern glauben will, die behaupten, er sei ein Avatar, eine lebende Inkarnation des Göttlichen, muß bei der persönlichen Begegnung mit dem Guru jeder selbst entscheiden. Es gibt keine institutionalisierte Hierarchie, die in solchen Dingen vermittelt. Die Heiligkeit eines Gurus bemißt sich an seinen Lehren und Taten und an dem Glauben seiner Anhänger. Eine Garantie gibt es natürlich nicht.

In der Geschichte der westlichen Beschäftigung mit der indischen Spiritualität wimmelt es nur so von Messiassen, die ihre Versprechen brachen, und von den enttäuschten Erwartungen ihrer Anhänger. Das unentbehrliche Werkzeug des spirituellen Touristen ist das kritische Urteilsvermögen. In den dreißiger Jahren lernte Paul Brunton auf seinen Reisen durch Indien auch Meher Baba kennen, einen Guru, der später im Westen eine große Gefolgschaft um sich scharte und nicht zögerte, sich als den „Avatar des Jahrhunderts" zu bezeichnen. Brunton kam zu dem Schluß, Meher Baba sei mit Sicherheit fehlgeleitet und möglicherweise sogar wahnsinnig.

Aber das wohl heilsamste und aufschlußreichste Beispiel für die seltsame Beziehung zwischen Ost und West ist die Geschichte von Krishnamurti. Als der englische Theosoph Charles Leadbeater im Jahre 1909 eines Tages in Adyar, in der Nähe von Madras, am Strand spazierenging, erblickte er einen zwölfjährigen Jungen, dessen Aura, wie Leadbeater zu spüren glaubte, „ohne ein Körnchen Selbstsüchtigkeit" war. Zusammen mit der Theosophin Annie Besant verbrachte Leadbeater die nächsten zwanzig Jahre damit, Krishnamurti zum neuen „Weltlehrer" aufzubauen – mit dem Ergebnis, daß Krishnamurti sich zuletzt von ihnen abwandte, weil er die für ihn vorgesehene Rolle nicht spielen wollte.

Wenn man heute denselben Strand entlanggeht, an dem Leadbeater seinen jungen Protegé entdeckte, werden Erinnerungen wach, und man gerät ins Grübeln über den unvergänglichen Glauben des Westens, daß die spirituelle Erlösung im Osten zu finden ist, und über die Enttäuschungen, die sich daraus ergeben können. Der strahlend weiße Sand erstreckt sich bis zum türkisfarbenen Meer, auf dessen Oberfläche die Sonne glitzert. Einige Jungen laufen am Wasser entlang, doch als sie den Fremden entdecken, kommen sie über den Sand geschlurft und beginnen ein Gespräch. „Wie heißen Sie?" wollen sie wissen. „Woher kommen Sie? Was machen Sie hier?" Der Name Krishnamurti sagt ihnen nichts. Die Idee, daß jemand aus dem Westen an diesen Ort reisen könnte, um Erleuchtung zu suchen, kommt ihnen unsinnig und absurd vor. Für sie ist der Westen das gelobte Land, wo es Motorräder und Popmusik gibt und Arbeitsplätze, mit denen man gutes Geld verdient. „Das ist mein Traum", sagt einer von ihnen.

Auch Krishnamurti ging in den Westen. Mit den berühmten Worten „Die Wahrheit ist ein unwegsames Land" und der Aussage, daß jeder Mensch seine Erlösung selbst finden müsse, lehnte er die ihm zugedachte Rolle als Weltlehrer ab und zog nach Kalifornien. Die Luft, sagte er, sei dort sehr viel sauberer.

Mick Brown ist der Autor des Buches „The Spiritual Tourist".
Er schreibt regelmäßig für das Londoner „Telegraph Magazine".

Bylakuppe
1996

Varanasi
1996

Varanasi
1996

Varanasi
1996

Pushkar
1998

Varanasi
1999

Varanasi
1996

Rishikes
1998

Varanasi
1999

Madurai
1999

Pushkar
1998

Haridwar
1998

Pushkar
1998

Madurai
1999

Haridwar
1998

Ramesvaram
1999

Varanasi
1996

Rishikesh
1998

Udaipur
1998

Haridwar
1998

Ramesvaram
1999

Haridwar
1998

Haridwar
1998

Manikoran
1998

Varanasi
1996

Pushkar
1998

Haridwar
1999

Ramesvaram
1999

Ramesvaram
1999

Varanasi
1999

Pushkar
1999

Udaipur
1998

Varanasi
1999

Mahabalipuram
1999

Haridwar
1998

109

Udaipur
1998

Varanasi
1999

Haridwar
1998

Madurai
1997

Varanasi
1999

Pushkar
1998

Haridwar
1998

Allahabad
1999

Published by: Kruse Verlag, Hamburg, Germany
Edited by: Peter Bialobrzeski, Hamburg
Translated by: Christine Madden, Regina Rawlinson
Design by: Astrid Borowski, Hamburg
Scans and reproduction by: Reproduktion Onnen & Klein, Hamburg
Printed by: Druckerei Weidmann, Hamburg

Kruse Verlag GmbH, Kampstr. 11, 20357 Hamburg, Germany,
Phone: 0049 40 4328246-0, Fax: 0049 40 4328246-12,
E-mail: info@KrusePublishers.com, www.KrusePublishers.com

Distribution in North-, South-, Central America, Asia, Australia and
Africa by: D.A.P./Distributed Art Publishers, 155 Sixth Avenue, 2nd floor,
New York, N.Y. 10013, Phone: 001 212 6271999, Fax: 001 212 6279484

Distribution in Europe, Asia, Australia and Africa by: IDEA Books,
Nieuwe Herengracht 11, 1011 RHK Amsterdam, Netherlands, Fax:
0031 20 6209299, E-Mail: idea@ideabooks.nl

Distribution in Germany, Austria and Switzerland by: Kruse Verlag

First Kruse Verlag Edition, 2000
Printed in Germany
ISBN 3-934923-04-6

agentur für **laif**
photos & reportagen

ACKNOWLEDGEMENTS

This book would not exist without my friendship to British writer Mick Brown. I am very grateful for his inspiration, and for stirring up my interest in spirituality. And of course for his wonderful essay about the Spiritual Tourists. Florian Hanig deserves an equally big "Thank You" for his essay, his interest and continuous support of my work. A big kiss to Astrid Borowski for the design. A cold beer to Peter Lindhorst for his tireless efforts to publish and distribute this book. More "Thank You's": Lars Kruse for his enthusiasm. Inge de Ridder for her love and patience when my thoughts were too far away. Henrik Spohler for his criticism and his wife Stefanie Clemen for her friendship and getting me back on the track when I saw no light at the end of the tunnel. Anja Jöckel for her belief in me and my work. Peter Bitzer and all the staff at "laif" in Cologne for their support. Everyone who is not mentioned for their curiosity, criticism and encouragement. All the magazines and companies on whose tickets I rode to India. Last but not least there are Eckart Hein, Lars Landmann and Matthias Rochner, who, way back in the eighties, shared the first smells and the enthusiasm of travelling the Asian roads with me. Without them, I would never have gone there.

I dedicate this book to the people of India, whose spirits are more than just a blurred shadow in these photographs. They have left a mark on my soul.

Peter Bialobrzeski, Hamburg, April 2000